TIGER TENNIS

Man of Mastery and the Competitive Mind

SVETOSLAV S. ELENKOV

Copyright © 2019
Svetoslav S. Elenkov
Tiger Tennis
Man of Mastery and the Competitive Mind
All rights reserved.

No part of this publication may be reproduced, distributed, or transmitted in any form or by any means, including photocopying, recording, or other electronic or mechanical methods, without the prior written permission of the publisher, except in the case of brief quotations embodied in critical reviews and certain other non-commercial uses permitted by copyright law.

Svetoslav S. Elenkov

Printed in the United States of America
First Printing 2019
First Edition 2019

10 9 8 7 6 5 4 3 2 1

TIGER TENNIS

Table of Contents

Before Birth 1
The Birth of the Claw 2
No Mercy 5
Risk Management 7
Retractable Claws 9
Fighting Style 11
Electric Attack and the Kinetic Chain 13
Fighting the Invisible Potential 15
Tiger's Breath (Conquering Nerves) 17
The Adaptive Hunter 20
Virtues of Asymmetry 23
Masters of Surprise 26
Information Harvester 28
The Yin and the Yang 31
More on Yin and Yang 34
Non-Verbal Communication 36
Importance of Environment 39
Mastery as a Burden 41
Relativity of Happiness 43
Extreme Realist (Eating the Dead) 45
A Lesson in Depersonalization 48
Generational Progress and DNA 50
Mental Domination 53
Interactions of the Beast 58
The Taunt 63
Hierarchy and Rank 65
Accepting the Animal 69

Before Birth

Asserting dominance, surviving, and thriving used to be the singular drive in the animal kingdom. But now that humankind has largely removed itself from the pressures of natural selection, it's become a struggle to balance our animalistic instincts with our newfound moral understanding of humanity and the world.

Since the dawn of civilization, organized sport has been an outlet for some of this destructive energy that might otherwise consume us. Having an outlet allows us to be polite to each other and compartmentalize our physical energy to the weight room, punching bag, basketball court, or football field. Instead of using our physical prowess to kill, steal, and oppress, we've unlocked a beneficial, healthy side of aggression. We've redesigned physicality to build respect among us and relieve us from the animalistic urge to destroy. Therefore, I argue that if one is to succeed at sports, it is useful to tap into the mind and habits of the most feared hunter in the world: the hunter that pays for failure with death and, if successful, is rewarded with complete dominance.

The Birth of the Claw

Just as a tiger is born, man enters a discipline blind, ignorant, clumsy—but ultimately determined. Important challenges such as learning to walk, communicate, or even play seem insurmountable to a young cub, but the razor-sharp learning structure of the feline mind allows for mastering these essential skills in a swift and methodical manner. We humans can learn from this.

Like us, tigers are very visual creatures. A cub, just like a baby, will spend most of its time observing the outside world and taking note of their parent's movements and behaviors. Young tigers internalize what they see, and try it out on their own. This isn't so very different from the way a human child learns and unlocks the world around them.

Tigers eventually try out their newly acquired skills in play. Again, this isn't any different than how humans would approach a discipline. A big difference between the learning curve of a tiger and a human is shame: A tiger will not experience shame when attempting new moves that they have internalized, nor will they experience shame in play. There is no shame in making a mistake or looking silly to their fellow cubs. There is no doubt or embarrassment to shackle their abilities in a cage built by bars of social pressure, judging peers, and family expectations. As kids grow older, their learning potential is sometimes curbed in the name of conformity or due to ineffective teaching techniques.

Knowing the difference between the way a tiger learns and the way a modern human learns reveals to us our shortcomings when striving for mastery in any discipline. **As often is the case, the unveiling of the truth informs the appropriate action when it is applied to one's situation.** If we are to achieve a learning method so sharp and swift as the one of a tiger, we must remove the shackles aforementioned—at least from our own mind.

Throughout this book, I will attempt to draw lessons from nature's most feared hunter, the tiger, and relate it to my own discipline of tennis and other human forms of mastery. Although I think this book will mostly relate to males in their 20's and 30's, as with any of my writing, it is my sincere hope that everyone who reads this can relate and learn from what I have to say. My wish is to effectively share my perspective regardless of who is on the other side of this page.

This will not be a comprehensive guide on how to become an excellent tennis player, as I've already written about this in another book called **Elite Tennis: A Guide**. This will also not be a humorous look at tennis culture or the characters that populate the courts around the world, as I've already written a book for that as well called **Clash of Tennis Personalities**. Rather, this book will take a deep look into the nature of our inner beast and take us on an exploratory journey into our connection with nature and our innate drive for mastery.

No Mercy

Mastery is a vital component of a tiger's survival. Tigers don't have social safety nets, community help, or distribution of labor among their population. They don't trade, they don't offer services, and they don't have other tigers helping them hunt (except for their mother, or in some cases father, and siblings for the first two years of their life). An adult tiger is solely responsible for themselves and their offspring. If they don't succeed, they die—and their family dies as well.

This mastery-or-die mentality is prevalent in tigers. They understand the risks, either consciously or subconsciously. A tiger can only live for two weeks without food. If they fail to hunt down a meal in these two weeks, they will die. **Likewise, the do-or-die mentality is a must for a man of mastery.** They sacrifice everything, and their pursuit of mastery is relentless. For modern man, survival isn't necessarily the key motivational factor, but rather it's the satisfaction of attaining true mastery. My speculation is that this thirst for mastery is an evolutionary hold-over; it is a trait that was selected out of necessity by nature. Whatever its source, there can be no denying it exists.

To find proof, one can simply look to the massive number of individuals who are not starving yet still strive for mastery every day.

There are numerous examples of this attitude among exceptional competitors. When interviewed, the exceptional masters of competitive disciplines often credit this way of thinking for their success. They describe it as a "no plan B," "everything on the line," "failure is not an option" type of mentality. It's not that these outliers aren't aware of the sacrifices and risks; they are fully aware of the stakes, but they sacrifice and risk nonetheless.

In order to pursue a career in tennis, for example, an aspirant must sacrifice their time and everything that comes with it—resources, education, relationships, and more. This career path carries risks of injury to the body and mind, unlike most other disciplines. The risk is great, but just like in a tiger's life, so too is the reward.

Risk Management

A tiger steps carefully and takes only calculated risks. There is no unnecessary energy expenditure unless it's relevant to their goal. There are no risky maneuvers unless the ratio of risk to reward is worth it. A tiger will not aimlessly sprint across the forest, because injury can mean death. Tigers do not have doctors or rehabilitation centers. If they break a tooth or a leg, it could mean the end. As a tiger lives their life, there are no fights, no games, and no thrills unless there is something to be directly gained from it.

The man of mastery adopts this calculating mind of a tiger. One must restrict or remove as much risk as they can from outside activities that do not contribute to the cause. For example, if one decides to become a tennis player, there will be no basketball, soccer, climbing, skiing, base jumping, mountain biking, or any other activity not geared toward helping the cause of becoming a tennis player. A tiger must have a singular focus to survive, as a man of mastery must have a singular focus to satisfy their thirst for excellence.

Examples of seemingly risky tiger behavior in the wild can be explained in tennis terms by the common strategy of "redlining." Redlining is a desperate act to achieve victory in the face of almost certain defeat. It is said that a tennis player is redlining when they pursue shots or tactics beyond their own skill or ability in an attempt to turn the tide in a tennis match. Similarly, a tiger will resort to such maneuvers in territorial fights or hunting in an act of desperation.

Risk is unavoidable. We swim in a sea of risk, and whoever succeeds in navigating it will eventually reach their destination. Those who do not realize this fact and swim carelessly will forever be lost, unless they follow or imitate someone else. In this case, they will reach a destination without understanding the methodology of how they got there—and perhaps without even a say in what that destination is. **A tiger, on the other hand, walks their own path and navigates their own territory. A man of mastery is self-aware and self-driven.**

Retractable Claws

Among many things, the king of the forest is a great judge. The feared claws of the tiger are retractable and used only when appropriate. **Likewise, a man of mastery must choose the right time to employ their weapons.** The claws come out when weakness and opportunity are sensed. Similarly, a masterful tennis player will go for the kill whenever the situation dictates. It is foolish to continuously pound murderous forehands from difficult situations, as the mistakes and injuries will pile up much faster than a tiger's chipped or broken claws. Such behavior could mean death from over-aggression.

This analogy of reserved aggression can be applied to many other disciplines. A boxer looks carefully for the perfect opportunity to deliver a punishing blow. Trying to continuously land high-energy strikes will simply tire them out and render them useless. A racecar driver does not always press the accelerator; brakes and control are just as important as speed. A basketball player will not shoot from anywhere on the court; rather, they will work hard to position themselves in a place where they can more reliably make their shot. The same can be said for soccer players and other high-level athletes.

In sports, "weapons" can be thought of as those maneuvers that are delicate and difficult to execute, or those that require great care and precision. The high cost of employing a weapon in competition is balanced out by the reward of causing great damage to the opponent, either physically or psychologically. Usually such strikes will be rewarded in the scoring system (if there is one). Proper discernment of when to use weapons is a trait of an experienced and attentive man of mastery.

Fighting Style

Tigers duel for territory or mating opportunities, and these duels can be (and often are) deadly. Unlike hunting for prey, the element of surprise is usually not present in these one-on-one duels for supremacy. A tiger must face his opponent and outmaneuver him, and there is no room for subtlety or subterfuge. There are many similarities and lessons that can be drawn between a tiger duel and a tennis match.

Like tennis, tigers fight in bouts—although these bouts last anywhere from a few seconds to half a minute. Because tigers are so explosive in their actions, their energy reserves get temporarily depleted. They need a relatively short period of rest in between bouts. Likewise, after an explosive serve-and-return sequence, a tennis player will take their time walking around, acquiring balls for the next point, or perhaps electing to "go to the towel" for further replenishment. It's not a good idea for a player to rush through the points without rest, unless it's part of a ploy to burn the opponent's energy faster than their own.

When the duel between two tigers begins, the typical reactionary response is a balanced paw spreading stance. A tiger will rise up and balance themselves on their hind legs while spreading their front paws and erecting their claws, preparing them for a strike. At this point, they usually bare their teeth, but they don't actually go for a bite unless the right opportunity arises. Most of the fighting is done, at least initially, with powerful and extremely swift claw strikes. The attacks are focused mainly on the head/neck area, but really any chunk of flesh they can manage to rip off is worth their swing.

Vision is paramount during and in between bouts. Both tigers stalk each other and never break eye contact. They are always ready to rise up into a quick exchange of blows. Similarly, when competing in tennis, eye contact with the ball must be always on point, but additional data can be collected without losing focus. This data is crucial for decision-making within or between points. In order for a player to acquire peripheral data, he must first automate his most used movements and strikes into a collection of associated and consecutive muscle activations. Only then will his attention be liberated to acquire peripheral information. The first step to such automation is the physical understanding and execution of the kinetic chain.

Electric Attack and the Kinetic Chain

Muscles are activated by electrical signals. They function as tiny on and off switches, which means that muscle is either activated or it isn't. This is a fact that eludes most people, including high-level athletes on a conscious level. Maximum power is achieved through timing and sequential muscle activation. Some call this the kinetic chain or kinetic wave.

The artistic and functional act of striking usually starts from the feet and legs, or sometimes from the hips. A successive activation of muscle groups ensures that the momentum already generated by other muscle groups is preserved and carried on to the next segment of a strike. A reversal of previously generated motion sometimes creates angular momentum that further accelerates parts of the body, which is sometimes called a "snap." Imagine the motion of a whip: the kinetic wave gives it the ability to carry energy along its length and benefit from the reversal of motion. A whip-wielder will swing one way just so they can reverse their swing with skillful timing.

Such motions take advantage of physics to create spectacular effects. A whip can break the sound barrier and produce a sonic boom if wielded with skill.

Understanding the physics of motion and developing skill for striking and throwing will serve you well in sports and in life. But remember: **just like an electrical switch, a muscle cannot be turned on if it's already activated.** You must approach a strike with relaxed muscles in order to activate them in a timely manner while drawing energy from your legs, hips, waist, and torso. A strike is a motion that involves the entire body. Putting effort into automating these physical principles will allow your mind to free up resources for strategy, focus, and the ability to constructively observe the situation. Don't be tricked into fighting an invisible tiger. Without automation of your physical actions, you will easily fall victim to pressures created by your opponent (which are "invisible" to you). They are invisible because by focusing on your own movement, you aren't aware of how your playing space is manipulated by the "invisible potential" described in the next chapter.

Fighting the Invisible Potential

Earlier I established how I believe tigers are masters of discernment. Here, I think we can draw an important lesson and apply to other sports. There is a situation during a game, match, duel, or a fight where a certain mental disadvantage comes into play. A competitor may say, "I can't go to my opponent's forehand because he punishes me every time." As a result, the playing field is now restricted to half the court. **The competitor in question is suffering from a disadvantage simply because of the potential damage that their opponent could do.**

I remember a tennis commentator once saying, "they lose to him simply because he is Federer." And this is correct. What this means is that Federer has time and again proven a set of situations where he masterfully punishes his opponents. When on the court, his opponents must try their best to play outside of this set of situations. This presents them with a very complicated problem to solve. A player taking on Federer may seem to swing wildly or "red line" without even being prompted to. Federer is forcing them to take on more risk than they otherwise would just with his presence—just by being

Federer. As Major J.W. Powell famously said, "A shadow is the sword of a great tree, and with this weapon it slays a thousand or a million."

Of course, here we refer to this in its metaphorical sense rather than its literal sense. The shadow in this analogy is the invisible potential that a great player "casts" upon their opponent. This shadow is responsible for restricting the opponent's options and slowly suffocating them out of life, or their ability to perform. A "great tree" indicates that a great competitor will use invisible potential to "slay millions" or defeat a great many others simply by means of their "shadow" that they cast during competition.

If a shadow is to be true and thick, it must be convincing and seemingly unyielding. A great champion wields his shadow with certainty. He experiences no doubt and nervousness when wielding such a weapon. A man of mastery is to overcome such challenges.

Tiger's Breath (Conquering Nerves)

Before and during competition, it is normal to experience nerves—if you are human. Your breath may speed up and become shallower, your hands might sweat, your stomach could get queasy, your lips may tremble, and your legs and arms may start to shake. However, for the tiger, this isn't a regular occurrence. The tiger's breath is always measured and congruent with their physical activity. Their inhalation and exhalation is unforced and unaffected by neurotic behaviors. A tiger's breath is the breath of a predator.

If you are struggling with nerves, it may be worth exploring a change in outlook and attitude. It may be of benefit to adopt the mindset of a predator. You could look at the competition as prey and not as a dangerous opponent. **Prey get nervous, not predators.** It isn't easy to tap into this animalistic way of looking at the world around you, and it may feel weird and strange at first. It will take practice, but place yourself in the eyes of the tiger and try to look at your competition from the perspective of an apex predator.

Yes, it's dangerous. There can only be one person on top of the food chain, and looking at the world as a predator will cause you to clash with other predators. It is clear what happens in the animal kingdom when two predators collide for dominance; the result is sometimes physical combat and even death. This isn't necessary in the civilized culture we live in today (hopefully), but for many hundreds and thousands of years humans underwent similar clashes on a regular basis.

As you go through the world without worrying if anyone is attacking you, harming you, competing against you, the body relaxes to the appropriate level. Competition becomes hunting, instead of being hunted, and the nerves disappear. It's important to note that relaxation does not mean a lack of alertness. A tiger on the hunt is just as explosive as his nervous prey in muscle reflex; the difference is that the explosiveness comes from an offensive mindset and not a defensive or reactionary one. A mental trick to keep yourself sane in a competition is to not think categorically about defeating or being defeated, but about how frequently or infrequently you defeat your opponent. There is no such thing as being defeated. Every point scored against you is nothing more than a lost opportunity or an unsuccessful attempt to defeat your opponent.

A less-nervous body will not only allow you to perform better and relieve your negative symptoms, it will also allow you to make better decisions, as your mind is not clouded by stress and pressure. The road to adopting a predatory mindset is challenging but worth the exploration. With enough practice and mastery, it's possible to switch this mindset on and off.

When you experience a confrontation with another predator, your conviction will be tested. It will become apparent if you've done the work and are able to stand in your own ability and presence of mind. If symptoms of nervousness arise, then your training is not complete. However, it may never be complete, **as the journey for mastery shows us that any path we take is an infinite climb, leaving only a trail behind that reminds us of how far we've come.**

The Adaptive Hunter

A tiger's jaw can apply 1,000 pounds of pressure, and a bite to the neck is the most commonly used maneuver to secure a kill. However, sometimes that method is inappropriate given the circumstances of the fight. At times, a tiger is brave enough to fight a crocodile, but a bite to the neck of a crocodile will yield poor results because of the thick scales protecting it. Instead, a tiger will first rake the eyes of a crock to blind them, then flip them on their backside and attack their relatively softer belly.

In tennis, it is a great idea to develop a specialty and then methodically defeat opponents with that weapon or tactic. However, there will be times where your main attack is countered, and a masterful player will be adaptive enough to recognize this situation and devise a response to it. For example, a tennis player's primary means of defeating opponents might be using punishing groundstrokes (very common), but if he is facing an excellent counter-puncher, the groundstroke line-drives just feed into the counter-puncher's strike zones and style of play. A master will recognize this and switch to heavy topspin lobs followed by approaching the net in order to neutralize the counter-puncher's strengths. When he does this, there will be no power for the opponent to feed off of. Moreover, extreme angles from the volleys will provide an impossible challenge compared to the angles that can be generated with groundstrokes.

Adaptation is not only a decision, but also a skill. The ability to adjust accurately and swiftly varies from person to person, but it is often directly related to experience. Having established adaptability as a skill, it can be trained and improved upon. How? Through constant observation and trial and error when attempting a change. For example, if a masterful player notices his forehands are finding the net, he can adapt and make the corrective action needed before the next attempt—he does not need to wait to make the change. **The speed at which we make decisions and how accurate they are will determine our skill at adaptation.**

There are many situations that require versatility. There is an ancient saying that portrays an expert as a jack of all trades AND a master of one(not none). **To truly excel in a discipline, you not only need to be exceptional with one style, but have sufficient skill level in other relevant styles and disciplines.** For example, an MMA fighter may be an expert striker, but will surely need some skill in ground combat, grappling, etc.

A great tennis player may have exceptional volleys, but she still needs to know how to perform ground strokes and other necessary skills. As I argue further, asymmetry in the skill of a competitor is a good thing. However, asymmetry does not mean isolation or complete disregard of all else besides the primary skill.

Virtues of Asymmetry

I've mentioned the specialization of the tiger and how they excel in a few very specific techniques in addition to having a signature method of securing a kill. A tiger is therefore **asymmetric** in their skills, lifestyle, size, and strength among other features relative to other animals. These asymmetric features are the reason why a tiger is most dominant in their environment.

As the tiger demonstrates, the virtue of asymmetry is an integral part of mastering any discipline. Let's take the inherent asymmetry of a tennis player as an example. Would a player be better off practicing serves with their left hand and right hand equally? Would one be able to master a left-handed serve as well as a right-handed serve? Would one be able to compete with the best in the world after only giving half of their practice time to each side? What if a bowler practiced bowling with their right arm half the time, and spent the other half of their practice with the left? Would they be as skilled of a bowler as someone who practiced with their right arm full-time?

The fact is that being a well-rounded competitor comes at the cost of not excelling in any one particular skill. Without having an edge over the opposition, failure is likely. One can make an argument that a competitor can be an exceptional generalist, and that's a fair point—that in itself can be an edge that not many others possess. However, from scouring the world of competition, this simply does not bare out. **Every champion has at least one skill they do better than anyone else in the world, which they then leverage to achieve victory.** This is why asymmetry is so important to mastering a competitive discipline.

The principle of asymmetry can be applied to many concepts, including time spent within and in between different disciplines. A golfer that spends more time honing their craft relative to other disciplines will achieve more success relative to a golfer that spends equal amounts of time between golf, tennis, basketball, reading, math, and, let's say, poetry. Sure, the latter version of the individual may be more well-rounded, an excellent generalist, and perhaps a better athlete overall—but he will not be a better golfer. Again, one can argue this point about generalists, but evidence disagrees.

As far as the practice of the tiger goes, unless the tiger is engaged in essential training, hunting, battling, caring for their family, or other essential functions, the tiger rests. **Resting seems to be of higher value than many other non-essential activities that can be done at any given time.** A man of mastery similarly employs the virtue of the "active rest technique." One does not rest from playing tennis by playing another sport. The regenerative process of the body and mind does not take place if not allowed, and advancement in the discipline of tennis is stifled.

I'm not advocating for the elimination of cross-training to develop athleticism, but goals and parameters have to be specified and focused upon the mastery of just one discipline. When cross-training, the risks have to be reduced and the practice session shouldn't be as rigorous as if you were training to specialize in that specific sport. For example, if I'm training to be a masterful tennis player, my cycling, boxing, or running regime should not be as rigorous as that of a professional cycler, boxer, or runner. The idea of cross-training is to extract maximum value for the least amount of risk and time spent within the alternative discipline.

To conclude, the asymmetry of the tiger's strength, explosiveness, fatal bite, and stalking intelligence leaves them unmatched in their environment. Furthermore, this asymmetry is leveraged in order to achieve success as measured by the continuation of their life and the establishment of themselves as the kings of their domain. A man of mastery should look to emulate this approach in his respective discipline to achieve his respective goals.

Masters of Surprise

A tiger has a natural adaptation that helps them disguise their massive bodies in their environment. Techniques like being able to suddenly stop their movement render them virtually invisible to their prey. (Some of the animals being hunted have poor eyesight when detecting immobile objects.) Enshrouding themselves in the unknown allows a tiger to close the distance to their target and deliver a surprise attack without having to use up large amounts of energy in a prolonged chase.

If an attack is unsuccessful, a tiger will retreat into the forest to look for another opportunity to prowl and strike. At times, a patient tiger will only need to make a single leap in order to snatch their future meal. Any information about the tiger's presence to their prey will reduce their chance of success.

Similar to the tiger, a wise competitor will conceal crucial information from their opponent. A tennis opponent does not know if you possess a specific shot until it is used; this information can include tendencies and subconscious patterns of play for a tennis player (or for other athletes like martial artists or boxers). Masterful tennis players and fighters alike will spend some time "feeling each other out" in the hopes of baiting their opponents into a reaction that reveals their instinctive moves, go-to shots, and defensive modes.

A conscious or subconscious examination of an opponent's tendencies can give a tangible advantage to a competitor. An element of surprise can often be the turning point in a competition. There is often that memorable moment in a chess match that both competitors agree decided or turned the match. Similarly, in other competitive sports and games like League of Legends, a "Baron steal" or a specific unexpected move in a team fight can mean the difference between victory or defeat. A recent notable example of this was AlphaGo's victory over the world's best Go champion. AlphaGo is a computer that made a seemingly unintelligent move which later revealed itself to be a crucial turning point that ultimately decided the outcome of the game. The surprise was not premeditated in this case, but was rather a calculated move. The point is that it came as a surprise to the champion Go player, and served as the pivotal point in the match. Intentional or unintentional, reality is reality.

The element of surprise, the mastery of the unknown, and the embracing of alternative paths have and will continue to serve competitors in the achievement of victory.

Information Harvester

A tiger's excellent information gathering adaptations receive little attention relative to their flashier features. However, it is important for us to discuss them, especially since we live in the age of information.

A tiger's night vision is nearly six times better than a human's. This ability is largely due to the increased reflectivity of a tiger's eye. The feline's hearing is also off the charts with their rarely matched infrasound detection ability. Not only are their information-gathering instruments finely tuned, but they also have impressive processing capabilities. A tiger can determine the age, sex, and fertility status of another just by detecting subtleties in urine markings.

Another overlooked information-gathering tool is a tiger's whiskers. Surrounded by blood capsules, this facial hair can detect shifts in air pressure and tiny movements as small as five nanometers, or 1/2000th the width of a human hair. This extreme sensing system is analogous to the rigorous environment awareness training that a man of mastery can undertake. In tennis, subtle differences in sand density between the paint used on the court and the paint used on the lines of the court can mean the difference between a successful winner or a torn shoulder (real example). But it need not even be that subtle—anyone can imagine how a gust of wind or a specific sun location can alter the conditions and outcomes of specific shots, points, and matches.

The reading of subtle hints is often subconscious in masterful competition, but it plays an important role in gathering and processing information. A tennis match may seem totally normal, but just a slight slip with the right foot when attempting to recover can mean the difference between defeat and victory. The slight slip will stick out like a fly on a wedding cake to a trained eye, and the inefficiency will be exploited repeatedly until a complete breakdown is reached.

When something irregular happens, a man of mastery will often do a double-take and focus on the event with the thought of "what just happened?" A quick processing of the event will reveal a path to victory, which can then lead to the exploitation of the noticed weakness. This moment can be analogous to a tiger spotting a limping deer hiding among a herd.

In order to hone this skill of spotting weaknesses—the hunter instinct—one can start consciously observing details about their opponent. What shoes are they wearing? What racquet are they playing with? Are they right-handed or left-handed? Are they fast or slow? How is their reaction time? Which stroke do they favor more? And so on. Once these questions begin to be answered automatically, a more detailed one can be asked in order to refine this information-gathering process.

As with any other activity, a balance must be struck between gathering information and acting on it. This art of balance between observation and action leads us to the very important conversation regarding the yin and the yang.

The Yin and the Yang

The ancient Eastern wisdom of striking a balance between two extremes has been interpreted and re-interpreted to apply to virtually all aspects of life. Tennis, competition, and the way of the tiger are no exception.

The study of yin and yang begins with the realization that it is not represented by a gray circle. **It is not the mixture and dilution of extremes that one should seek; rather, it is the dance between extremes that yields the best results and truly reveals itself as the way in each discipline.** The ancient symbol is represented by opposing concepts that are intertwined with one another: white and black, light and darkness, order and chaos.

In tennis, it is easy to get lost in a specific idea of how one should achieve victory. Some players may find a more defensive style to "work for them." Some players may only rely on offense. The truth is that a player needs to wield both aggressiveness and passiveness with skillful discernment. The two extremes must be employed with appropriate timing and strength in order to achieve success. Understanding this interplay is critical.

If we examine a tiger's movement, we will notice the balance of extremes. When the predator advances unseen toward their prey, they move slowly and methodically as if to appear passive or even invisible. Only when the opportune moment reveals itself does the tiger pounce. Standing still and inactive is the inverse extreme of a powerful and explosive lunge at maximum acceleration.

A tiger can balance extreme inaction with extreme action, and I argue that a man of mastery will benefit from doing the same in competition. A defensive style of play and aggression have their time and place in a match. For example, it is not a good idea to hit fast, powerful, flat shots from a considerable distance behind the baseline, but these same shots could serve a player well from within the tennis court. Similarly, loopy topspin shots may not be appropriate from within the service line, but very effective from beyond the baseline. These are simple examples that may have exceptions, but the principle is the same throughout play. One should not look to hit every shot with moderate topspin and a fair amount of drive (gray circle), but instead devise a custom-tailored shot for every situation by taking into account the two possible extremes (yin and yang).

This principle of balancing extremes can, of course, be applied to all other aspects of training to become a man of mastery.

Another example of this is the training itself. A vigorous and exhausting session balanced by deep regenerative rest will yield the best results. Not only is this true on an intra-day schedule, but on a drill-to-drill and point-to-point basis as well as on a scale of periodization (read **Elite Tennis** for more on this topic). If we observe some of the best tennis players in the world, we will notice extreme effort during a point balanced out by minimum effort between points. Some competitors are even called sluggish or lazy by commentators and fans because of such behaviors. Clearly, such comments only show ignorance.

Striking a balance isn't always as two-dimensional as it may seem. For example, a man of mastery must find a balance between effort and rest as well as balance between effort and injury. If one's body is pushed too hard, the effort could lead to unpredicted injuries that not only harm the competitor but also delay further practice and development. A man of mastery must also strike a balance between effort and endurance, distribution of effort between strength and accuracy, and other aspects related to effort. It is not an easy task to manage one's activity masterfully. This process is often unconscious, but once brought to conscious attention, it is possible for a man in training or competition to make adjustments in order to improve training quality and performance results.

More on Yin and Yang

The age-old struggle is that between order and chaos. What is important to note here is that there is a seed of order in chaos and a seed of chaos in order. When our world, or environment, or activity is completely chaotic, we yearn for that speck of order that can bring some structure to our lives. We attach ourselves to it, we cherish it, grow it, and perhaps one day it overcomes us—then our activity, or goals, or life becomes so structured and static that it chokes us out and deadens our being. In that moment of overbearing order, we desperately seek that speck of chaos that brings the promise of destruction and liberation of old restrictive systems. We cherish and grow that speck of chaos until it inevitably becomes our life, our goals, our selves, our everything.

Similarly, in competition, there is a very real cycle of hope and despair. If not identified, understood, or acknowledged, this cycle can throw us into desperation, confusion, and hopelessness. At times, the regime, the training, the lifestyle, and the work can slowly squeeze the life out of us, and the seed of destruction sprouts in our mind. It grows, nurtured by our thoughts and ideas until one day it reaches critical mass and prompts an impulsive change.

The explosion can leave us stranded alone in the desert of aimless thoughts, forever wandering in search for our seed of order. **This process of change isn't good or bad—it just is. It's up to us to harness its power, cultivate its creativity, maximize its impact, or minimize its harm. It's up to us to balance it, expedite it, or learn from it. It's up to us to induce it, suppress it, strike it down, or empower it.**

Non-Verbal Communication

Humans rely on words to convey their thoughts, ideas, and mental or physical states. However, a tiger will go through their entire life without saying a word. They will hunt, mate, raise their family, pass on information and skills, and thrive without any verbal communication. How do the young cubs know where to stand and when? How do they know where the line between playing and seriousness is? How do two adult tigers resolve conflict without talking it out?

Bewildered by the power of non-verbal communication, one day I made it an experiment to teach tennis to a player using no words—and the result surprised me. I was just as effective, if not more effective, as a teacher using only gestures and physical guidance than I was when teaching verbally.

I believe there is an animalistic communicator inside all of us. I believe it's the same language that one uses to communicate with their body. If this language of action is mastered, it will unlock fluid and necessary communication between mind and body that a man of mastery requires. **Learn to communicate with yourself in a non-verbal way to unlock the athletic potential of your body—and perhaps even more.**

Non-verbal communication is most useful for physical self-control, which includes movement, emotion, and the control of physical symptoms like anxiety, fear, panic, pain, and so on. The applications are nearly limitless.

The techniques used to improve your physical language are numerous. Let us instead focus on a few examples of how said language manifests in our daily lives in order to better understand it. When brushing our teeth, we usually pick up the brush with one hand and the toothpaste with the other. Our body will do this by default even without us thinking about it. However, one day we may decide for the sake of experiment to switch hands. At this moment we are issuing a command, a type of communication to our body. There are no spoken words, no written commands, no pictures, no emails, no sign language, but yet our body understands the communication. The conversation doesn't end there. The feeling of awkwardness whenever the toothbrush is picked up and used is our body's way of telling us that something is not normal. We can choose to listen to that communication, or we can choose to ignore it, but it exists.

If a man of mastery is to improve, physical changes will need to occur. The better he speaks the language of his physical body, the better equipped he will be to deal with sudden as well as gradual changes in competition, including taking physical actions, learning physical motion, and finding a constructive balance between effort and recovery. Being fluent in the physical language will make you more adaptive.

Importance of Environment

A change in the environment can be detrimental and deadly. Many generations of evolutionary pressures have produced the wonder of nature that is the tiger. An adaptable creature, the magnificent hunter of the jungle stands out as the apex predator in his environment.

Similarly, if a competitor is to advance to an apex individual in their field, he must place himself in a conducive environment. It will be very difficult for a lawyer to advance to the highest level of his discipline by surrounding himself with artists and basketball players. The people one surrounds themselves with aren't the end of the story, either. Location matters. Does this lawyer have access to all the information he needs? Is he using the best studying techniques that have been proven successful over the years? Will he need to reinvent the wheel all on his own? Can anyone today imagine a lawyer becoming the best in their field without using the internet or a computer?

The advantage of staying on the cutting edge of a discipline is a significant advantage. Finding the right environment for development is an essential ingredient to success and dominating the competition. A tiger will not be the apex predator in New York City or in the middle of the ocean (although tigers make decent swimmers for being cats), but put that same tiger in a jungle or rainforest, and chances are he will reach the top of the food chain.

It is important to note that abrupt changes in the environment can stifle progress. Just as a tiger will need much time to adjust to life in the city (if he ever does), a competitor will need time to adjust to their new environment. Sometimes uprooting a rising talent and dropping them in different environments can be either detrimental or a boon for their success.

Mastery as a Burden

Many are the stories of kings with heavy crowns. Those who have been there have told the story. Our thirst for mastery is a blessing and a curse. The tiger is on top of the food chain, but it takes endless effort to stay there. Their huge body mass takes a great amount of food to maintain, which means that many difficult choices have to be made. The energy is precious and must be deployed in the right manner; otherwise their body is starved and the fall from the top is imminent.

Over-exhaustion of a large hunter from chasing prey without success can be deadly. A king's mistake in a territorial dispute can also mean death. Miscalculations may be the difference between being at the top or falling from it. As the old saying goes: "The higher you are, the harder you fall."

This isn't to say that a man should not pursue mastery; rather, it is to say that he needs to understand the risks and set realistic expectations. It's easy to maneuver the world from underneath the wing of someone or something else, and it is certainly not the same thing as spreading your own wings. It's different to be the one taking the risks and protecting yourself (and maybe others) against what the world throws at you.

In other words, it's easy to walk behind the man with the machete in the jungle. However, you'll always be walking in someone else's path, which means you'll always be second—and never be the king.

Understanding this lesson shouldn't act as a disincentive, nor should it act as a warning sign. It is merely meant to accentuate that the **process is what matters, not the destination. There is no destination.** One should not declare victory even when they summit the mountain. As any great champion will tell you, staying there is harder than getting there. Staying there requires even more rigorous focus and execution toward continual improvement.

A world number one tennis player is a few bad meals from losing his top ranking. A bad night of sleep, a sudden cold, or an equipment malfunction could be the difference between being on top and not being on top. Champions live on the edge of failure, and they fend it off daily.

Relativity of Happiness

Putting emphasis on "the process" is important, because it relieves us of the pressure to achieve happiness. One advantage tigers have over humans is the lack of such pressures. Culturally we are pushed toward happiness. We seek happiness. We make our lives revolve around happiness. But happiness is just a fleeting emotion and not really a state of being. Sometimes the feeling can persist for a long time and become a state, but usually these states of being are associated with depression or manic states. It's unusual for people to live in a state of euphoria with disregard for sober facts and decision-making. Just as prolonged euphoria is unusual and a sign of worry, so too is prolonged depression. **A state of contentedness will yield a more objective result that grounds itself in our animalistic nature and reality.**

Just as happiness is fleeting, it is also relative. This is very important to keep that in mind when you embark toward a goal that requires you to endure hardships. Once these hardships become part of your daily routine and way of life, they no longer require so much willpower and motivation as when they are first introduced.

The mind and body adjust, and in time it becomes possible to experience happiness from just resting after a long day of training. At one point in the past you may have been dissatisfied with resting. It may have brought you sadness and despair. But now, it brings happiness and joy.

The lesson here is that although happiness is great, the **primary driving factor in achievement isn't happiness or the potential for happiness—it's desire (or thirst)**. Basing future plans on how happy you will be while working toward a goal is going to yield inconsistent results. Happiness is only a byproduct of things going relatively well for a period of time. We cannot base our lives on something so unstable. The burning desire and thirst is a much better motivator. As long as this motivator is based in reality, there will be progress.

Extreme Realist (Eating the Dead)

It's a rare occurrence, but a male tiger will sometimes kill the offspring of a prospective mate (but this is more common in lions). This frees up the mother from the burden of caring for her cubs and makes her available for mating again. On an even rarer occasion, the mother might eat her own dead cubs if food is in short supply.

Now, I'm not advocating we feast on our dead family members. As always, the goal is to draw the analogy and apply the lesson to competition and mastery. What I see in this behavior is extreme realism. The mother immediately accepts that all the care she has given her young up to that point is now lost. With few other options, she chooses to do the most practical thing at the time. To prevent starvation, and have a better chance of new offspring, she chows down on her dead cubs for nutrition.

This attitude of immediate acceptance is sometimes necessary and useful in competition or even in life. For example, if a match is lost, there is no time machine. Nothing we do now will change the fact that a match has been lost.

There may be lessons learned, and productive discussions to be had, but what's done is done. The only way now is forward. The focus needs to be on "what now?" What is the best course of action from this current point in time? Is it to rest the fatigued muscles and regenerate? Is it to review the tapes and extrapolate the lessons? Is it to adjust the practice routine and competition schedule?

Eating the dead can also take on a different meaning that yields a different lesson. In economics, there is a process called Creative Destruction. It's a process of devaluation, destruction, or modification of old structures and ways of life in order to make way for newer, more efficient means of getting things done. Similarly, a man must sometimes "eat the dead" and consume what is within him or around him to salvage the energy needed to build newer and better structures.

A more materialistic example of eating the dead is the change of equipment. Sure, the type of strings and racquet one uses is important, and a bond must be formed for effective play, but changes must be made as the technology is advanced and improved. Even if it's emotionally tough, it might be time to salvage what is left from the old gear and have it be sold or destroyed in order to make way for new and better tech.

A more personal and spiritual example of eating the dead is a change in one's philosophy. It's much more painful to change the way one thinks about and views the world, and by extension, their attitude toward a goal or vision. I can share a personal example here. At one point I thought that all that mattered in order to become a better tennis player was more practice and better practice. I refused to even consider alternative views on the matter. This stubborn behavior led me to an 8-hour practice day, an overworked body, a fragile mental and physical state, and a broken back. Only then did it become clear to me that I was wrong about my views.

For some, like me, it was tough to disassociate emotions from events. It was tough to change and take a cold objective look at my situation. I needed to use a more sober lens to view the world. I needed to depersonalize myself from my views.

A Lesson in Depersonalization

A tiger can be caring at times and brutal at others. Killing cubs for reproductive purposes, killing prey to feed, or killing other tigers in territorial disputes is on the menu for the large feline's everyday life. The ability to mentally navigate through these merciless experiences is yet another reason why the tiger sits where he sits—at the top of the food chain.

Again, I'm not advocating that we become psychopaths. However, depersonalization is a healthy tool in every human's life. It is the ability to separate emotion and personal attachment from events and objects in the external world. It can help deal with past trauma, and it can also be useful to competitors in their pursuit of mastery. Let me share a personal example of how I was able to rationalize and limit my empathy for my tennis opponents for the better (for both me and my opponents).

As a young tween, I would sometimes compete against kids who were not up to my skill level. It was a common practice for me to "give" them a game or two during the match so they didn't feel as bad about losing. This was an unhealthy practice. It was dishonest, and it did no one any favors. I then really analyzed this in my mind. If I intentionally made even just a few mistakes per match, I wasn't giving the honor of presenting myself to the best of my ability to my opponent. The lessons that my opponent and I learn from such a match will not be truthful—and not nearly as useful as if I play my best. The observations we make about the differences in our ability will be skewed, unrealistic, and may lead us to false conclusions about future expectations. These expectations can be the cause of subpar training routines, tournament schedules, a degradation of attitudes, and ultimately a hindrance for both of us as we seek to progress.

This is just one example of how "emotional blunting," or depersonalization through reasoning, can work in a positive manner for all parties involved. Just as empathetic limitations can work with opponents, they can also work with events like lost opportunities, and traumatic experiences. **Limiting emotional attachment can help a man of mastery move on and make rational choices that help his future instead of entangling himself in the past.**

Generational Progress and DNA

Often a dominant tiger is the product of successful survival tactics that include sufficient hunting skills and physical ability. Traits that are relevant for the success of a tiger have a good chance of being passed on to their progeny, and over many generations, gradual improvements are made. The structure of a tiger does not only change intergenerationally, however, and nor is the rapid development reserved only for them. It's also possible for the physical appearance and tendency/behavior of a human to morph throughout the duration of one's life.

A human can end up looking like a bodybuilder if they adopt a certain lifestyle, and his body morphs based on the physical activity that dominates his life. Sometimes you can easily guess an athlete's chosen sport just by their appearance. A broad-backed man with smoothly defined muscles is likely a swimmer. A man with large muscle mass and definition on his legs may indeed be a soccer player, and so forth.

The more specialized the body of a competitor becomes, the easier it will be for him to maneuver through his field of choice. As a man evolves, his body builds pathways to develop specific physical attributes in a more efficient way. This exact process then gets encoded into the DNA of the next generation to an extent (There is debate in the scientific community about the generational transferability of DNA methylation. Observation of life outside the lab seems to confirm there is at least some, or at the very least something else is in play). With the exploitation of these paths, a more perfect competitor can be developed over time. The interplay across generations of building physical attributes and exploiting genetic advantages along with the passing down of knowledge and experience can lead to truly spectacular results. But should we try it?

The concept of intergenerational polishing isn't new, but it bumps into many ethical barriers and questions. It's wise for one to consider these topics before forming conclusions about different courses of action. We should remember that the journey toward mastery is what's important, and not achieving mastery itself. This elusive achievement of mastery doesn't carry any markers of completion. We'll never be able to tell if we've attained it. Mastery itself isn't worth compromising principles and morality.

The goal is to satisfy the thirst for mastery without it compromising our integrity as reasonable individuals.

Although I explore the similarities between us humans and the majestic felines, there are still important differences. Perhaps it's a good time to take a moment and briefly explore the most important one. Humans are a much more social species with the ability to reason, and therefore have the burden and responsibility of morality. If I know that there is a child stuck in a basement, I now have the knowledge of that fact, as well as the ability to reason that he will starve if I don't help him. This obligates me to help, or I will more or less be committing murder by leaving him be. A tiger will not be able to reason through the situation, and therefore we hold it to a different standard. We can't blame a tiger for just walking by and not taking action, but we can blame a human.

Although the mental faculties of humans and tigers have taken different evolutionary paths, there is still much to learn from a tiger's mind. A tiger thinks offensively and understands the mental state of his prey. With such insight, he's able to mentally dominate his environment.

Mental Domination

A tiger, knowing that he can't outrun his deer prey in a sprint, will sometimes use mental tactics to close the gap. Once noticed by the deer, a tiger's chances of catching up to his meal plummet. The deer is faster and can last longer in a prolonged chase. The element of surprise has been lost, so a new path to success must be employed. An act of passivity follows. The discovered tiger might turn around and pretend to walk back in shame, hungry and knowing that he lost the opportunity. But did he? Once the deer loses sight of the predator for a second and basks in their ability to outsmart the killer—SNATCH! The tiger launches unseen from a nearby bush. A swift and quiet maneuver allows him to attack from the shadows.

Acting one way and doing the opposite is a well-known maneuver in almost any competitive activity. In poker, a player may act very conservatively to build up a reputation on the table only to bluff on a crucial hand. A boxer might act defeated in order to lure his opponent into thinking the end is near and waste his energy on intense yet unsuccessful attacks.

A tennis player may pretend to be a passive retriever in order to lure his opponent in feeling safe after floating a ball mid-court. Once the ball is attacked, and the point is lost, the opponent is left in dismay.

The secret to mentally manipulating your opponent is simplicity. A complex maneuver will not work to lure your opponent into wasting energy or making unintelligent moves, as they will not think they have outsmarted you. To illustrate this point, I've come up with the "Starbucks Analogy."

If you go to Starbucks one day and upon being welcomed you order a medium hot chocolate with no whip, chances are the barista will smile and make it for you without much fuss. If the next day, you arrive in the exact same manner and order a medium hot chocolate with no whip again, the barista will smile, make it for you, but this time perhaps make a mental note. If the third day you come around, he may ask "Medium hot chocolate with no whip?" "Well, yes, haha!" you say with a wholesome smile, giving away that you've been read clearly by the barista. He smiles, makes your drink, and both of you go on your way.

The next day you may come and confirm his bias again. "Thank you, I really appreciate it." However, one day the barista will see you coming and already be making your drink for you. At this very moment, you've got him. Through acting and establishing an easily readable pattern, you have lured him into putting in effort and work where there may be none. You walk in the store this day and he says, "Here you go sir, I've started your hot chocolate. It will be done in a second." "Oh, no!" you say, "I need two tall americanos today, please!" The barista is disappointed and befuddled. Left in dismay, he now has to throw away the chocolate drink he has prepared in order to work on your (strange) new order.

The reason why the barista has wasted his effort is because he thought he could read your pattern. If you came into Starbucks the first day and ordered a grande caramel frappuccino, an iced coffee the next day, a white mocha frap the next, and so on, the barista would always stand ready to make any random drink you desire. There will be no wasted effort, just an intense focus on receptivity. Something similar happens in a tennis match.

For instance, if you decide to "hit to his backhand" for the first few games, what will happen is that your opponent will make an adjustment. He will start moving his ready position slightly toward his backhand side. After a period of time, predictability will be so high that he may forego the ready position and split-steps altogether. It may become more effective for him to simply begin to move toward his backhand at the sight of your swing. This way, you are establishing yourself as a predictable, one-dimensional fool of a player. Now that your opponent has a bias in regard to your playing pattern, you can switch it up at will to leave your opponent in dismay. He thought he had outsmarted you, but now he slowly realizes that he was the one who was outsmarted. Sometimes this may result in ego barriers that prevent reality from sinking in, and the bias toward the backhand side may persist for the remainder of the match. It really depends how conscious your opponent is about what's going on. They may never adapt again and keep opening up their forehand side repeatedly. If they do realize what has happened, you can now craft your next move with an information advantage over your opponent. Perhaps they now take you for an intelligent player, and a more randomized approach to shot selection will work wonders as they struggle to find a pattern in your gameplay—even though there may be none! **You must create a pattern so you can break it.**

A more complex play style will not result in such a mental victory. If I vary my shot selection and pick different placements, spins, and power generation on every shot, my opponent will adapt and remain neutral and in his assumptions and more alert in his preparations. I'll be forced to execute more and more difficult shots in order to put my opponent in trouble and off-balance. This may result in more errors on my side, and a victory for my opponent. This is akin to a tiger trying to outsprint a deer in the open, or you trying to catch the barista off guard with a random drink. It's an uphill battle and will not result in mental domination.

I remember a moment during my competitive days as a junior at the age of nine when I got outsmarted by a 10-year-old. My opponent successfully hit a drop-shot on me a couple of times in the first game. I adapted to the strategy, and for the rest of the match I started running up every time he was about to slice his backhand. To my surprise, he would hold the shot—making it obvious he was slicing—only to place it deep behind me as I ran forward. I repeatedly chased after a drop shot that never materialized. I was so confused that by the time I figured out what was happening, the match was over. Had my opponent randomized his slice placements instead of duping me with a simple and predictable pattern, he may not have won as many points this way—or even the match.

Acting and faking your opponent in a simple way will most often elicit a false sense of security and overconfidence that will impair their ability to react effectively and think strategically.

Interactions of the Beast

The tiger engages in various interactions that help him maneuver through his environment. The interactions may be interspecific (i.e., between various different species) or intraspecific (i.e., between other tigers). Having an understanding of these interactions might give a competitor an idea of what he can expect on his journey. Breaking down the interactions and being able to categorize them will let him know what he can expect.

Mutualism

There is very little mutualism in a tiger's life, but what mutualism does exist can be found in play. As cubs are growing and honing their skills, they will often play-fight. This benefits all of the participants, which is the definition of mutualism.

In the tennis world, as well as other sports, it's common to find competitors (especially in the lower ranks) banding together in groups in order to benefit from sparring with each other. Although this strategy can work for a period of time as the players climb the ranks together, eventually there can only be one #1, so the bond naturally breaks.

This type of dynamic is also seen in the world of the tiger, as brothers and sisters separate in order to compete against each other for territory, mating rights, and food.

Non-Interference

Tigers are very territorial animals. They mark their territories and try their best to stay out of each other's areas (out of mutual respect). The defined borders help with conflict prevention and ultimately help the propagation of the species by maximizing the available hunting grounds.

In the world of sports, there are many different academies, training grounds, and teaching methods that do not interfere with one another in a positive or a negative way. The products of these different organizations may eventually compete, but it is possible for them to co-exist and be unaffected by one another simply because of their geographical separation. A tennis academy in Oklahoma isn't likely to interact with an academy in Nicaragua. However, in some cases these organizations may compete with one another if the quality of one is so high that it sucks away potential talent from another. In much the same way, many of today's best players are trained without interference from competitors until they eventually must compete.

For example, Roger Federer would not pack up and start training in Rafael Nadal's training grounds. They won't share the same coach, philosophy, schedule, and geographical location. Tennis players may be friendly and respectful toward each other, but if fierce competition is the game, they will not be friends, or likely to share any resources.

Competition

Competition is a defining feature of the tiger. He competes for food, territory, mating privileges, and other limited resources. Usually most of the competition is decided through brute force and fighting skill. However, sometimes politics and subterfuge come into play.

Likewise, a man of mastery thrives in competition. Luckily, men do not have to fight or seriously injure themselves in order to resolve conflict or attain a place in the hierarchy anymore. Food is easily secured, territorial disputes are decided through monetary means, and mating privileges are no longer secured through aggression and physical combat.

Some of these dynamics manifest themselves in the world of tennis. Equipment and food can (arguably) be secured easily. If a player cannot secure proper equipment and nutrition, he will be at an extreme disadvantage. There is competition for training grounds and trainers, but again, that is mostly decided by money. And thankfully mating two tennis players isn't necessarily a requirement for the development of a champion, so mating privileges are irrelevant. In modern society, aggression and combat is reserved purely for on-court competition where it can be honed and focused. This on-court battle serves goals that are hierarchical as well as mastery-oriented. Competition is a good way to showcase how far into his mastery one has risen.

Predation

Besides the obvious acts of predation, a tiger will sometimes choke out resources from another. It isn't uncommon for one to encroach on a rival's territory in the search for food. This act shrinks the possible hunting ground of a rival and slowly starves him. Since one individual benefits at the expense of the other, this relationship is defined as predatory. Sometimes these acts can turn into a territorial dispute resulting in a fight. In such imbalanced fights, the prey may resort to unconventional or "redlining" tactics in order to survive.

This analogy can be applied to in-game mechanics as well as environmental ones. During a tennis match, a predator might sniff out a weakness in his opponent and exploit it all the way to victory. Some examples are limping, a weak backhand, or poor skill at the net. A predator will make his opponent run as much as possible, hit often to his opponent's backhand, or frequently pull his opponent up to the net in order to exploit his weakness. This is, believe it or not, the more honorable and healthy version of predation in sport.

In an environmental sense, a predator might engage in psychological warfare with a potential competitor. A competitor's access to food or training grounds could be hampered by use of politics and connections. The competitor's mental stability could be rattled by using underhand tactics. I remember a story about two popular MMA fighters who had a fight coming up. One of them booked the training facilities around the area where the fight was going to happen and, in doing so, restricted his opponent's ability to practice. This event was not only a physical undermining, but a psychological one as well.

I'm not advocating that we must engage in politics or underhand tactics to prey on our potential opponents. This is meant to make you aware of what's out there and to help you prepare for potential events. The level and type of response is subjective, and each person must figure out on their own. We must, again, remind ourselves that all analogies break at some point. Humans are not literally tigers. We have principles and culture. We are civilized and guided by the philosophy of our minds.

The Taunt

Sometimes a tiger will use a taunt like displaying his teeth in order to prevent an escalation of a situation. The taunt is meant to say: "If we are to engage in battle, I'm prepared and it will be bloody. So it's best for both of us that we don't even attempt it."

The way taunting works in sport is by the display of skill or ability in a masterful way for a short period of time. One example is displaying the ability to hit a short slice serve if your opponent starts backing up after your hard flat serve. Performing the slice serve sends a very valuable taunt to your opponent. If performed skillfully, the taunt will prevent your opponent from staying too far back, and it will help you avoid a battle that neither of you want to fight—attempting slice serves for the rest of the match. Neither one of you wants to involve yourselves in such a match.

Another example could be performing a series of hard putaways or risky out-of-the air volleys after your opponent starts to consistently lob the ball to the baseline. This taunt shows your opponent that you can handle the lob, so now you don't have to. Your opponent will stop.

Taunts don't have to take the form of a skill. A taunt could be what one does after performing a skill in order to accentuate it. One example may be a sudden pause of movement after a very accurate passing shot or a drop-shot. This short "flex" sends a message of "don't you dare come in against me again," or, "you better respect my drop shot and stop hiding behind the baseline." The pause of movement can take many forms. It could take the form of a pose being struck by the player, or it could be just a little bit of unbroken eye-contact after the shot is executed while remaining still. Being still is important, because it demonstrates perfect balance and hints at the replicability of the shot. In other words, the pause shows a signal that what just happened was not an accident.

Having the skill and ability combined with "the pause" can send messages to your opponents that form a certain respect for your game. This way, you don't need to use cheap gimmicks and tricks, and a more skillful and authentic competition will ensue. Mastering the taunt will allow you to play your game more often and, therefore, win more often.

Hierarchy and Rank

Among tigers as well as men there is always a rank. Actions (either subtle or overt) and taunts are the tools used to determine the rank of each individual. In order to advance in rank, a male will often have to dominate another (or many others) in a physical or mental contest. Sometimes the competition for rank can escalate to physical altercation. Other times, the competition stays unresolved and the ranking conflict lasts for many years.

The overall rank takes many factors into account, but the most valued are potential accomplishments and results. When two or more individual males first meet, there will be a slew of conscious or subconscious tests for each to get a "feel" for the other. Judging by the responses of the tests, a rank will be applied. This rank helps predict future behavior and establish someone as a threat, friend, competition, or foe.

A person must be able to withstand verbal and physical attempts at de-ranking in a new setting. He needs to either establish himself as dominant, or at the very least respectfully suspend the battle over a territory he doesn't care much for. Suspending the ranking process is usually temporary or maintained through distance and constant tension. For example, if you go to a party and some guy challenges you to an arm-wrestling contest, it's often a subtle subconscious or conscious test for rank—no matter how playful and innocent the challenger seems. Your actions from here will be noted by everyone at the party. Do you politely reject the challenge? Do you accept the invitation readily? What if you lose? Do you accept the challenge and play it off as a weird thing to do while losing "on purpose?" Do you "see through" the challenge and escalate it to a real fight if the arm wrestler really desired competition? Do you instead propose a different activity? Do you ignore the challenge and skillfully steer the conversation in a different direction? Your rank will be determined by everyone at the party by your actions, your appearance, your achievements, and your potential achievements.

In sports, rank is often relevant going into a competition. You may hear a player complain, "But, he is the #1 seed. I have no chance." Or they'll say, "He's beaten Mr. So-and-so, and therefore I have no chance." Or they might say, "He's only a low-level player, I'll have no issues beating him." This type of mentality is very natural but also quite harmful to success in sport. It appeals to "rank" and leads to the overestimation or underestimation of your opponent's ability and often to a mental breakdown in disbelief during or after a match.

In the event that a match goes unexpectedly bad against an opponent you perceive as lower rank, you may panic and change play styles. The change will most often be detrimental and cause you to lose the match. Panic and "choking" are often associated with moments of disbelief. In addition, you may also get upset, and this could cause you to be unable to focus on the task at hand.

In the event that a match goes unexpectedly well, panic and disbelief will again set in, causing you to self-sabotage and revert the score back to your previously expected "natural order." In your subconscious mind you might start to think: "But, he's so much higher rank than me, I shouldn't be winning right now." Focusing on who should or shouldn't be winning is taking focus away from the match. Also, if you perceive a player as superior, you may not try as hard. "What's the point? He'll win anyway."

There are a couple of methods of circumventing the natural phenomenon of rank. One way is to make yourself believe that you are indeed the best, or eventually will be the best, and it's only a matter of time until you are. The second method, however, is the one I prefer. It is to remove belief of any kind from your thinking. Let a competitive event be an exhibition.

Focus on matching up your strengths with your opponent's weaknesses, be efficient, give it 100% effort in the most intelligent way you can, and let the chips fall where they may. The feel and attitude of this judgment-free mental approach and philosophy is perhaps best captured by Stan Wawrinka's tattoo, which reads: "Ever tried. Ever failed. No matter. Try again. Fail again. Fail better." The quote is credited to poet Samuel Beckett.

It shouldn't matter if you are competing against an unknown player with poor technique or Roger Federer. The process should always be the same and the level of focus should be unchanged. Having this attitude will prepare you for the unknown as you go into every match with an open mind that is fundamentally unclouded by expectation and belief.

Accepting the Animal

You are ready. You've sharpened your claws. You've calmed your breath. You've fought invisible adversaries and mastered surprise. You've understood ancient wisdom, climbed ranks, and eaten the dead. You've gained an intimate understanding of your inner animal that will give you clarity, unity, direction, peace, and a competitive edge like no other. Champions in physical trials rise and fall, but defeat and victory is just a fleeting moment in a timeless story. Failure and success are irrelevant to the act of testing yourself against the world. Winning is not an event but a journey. Just as a caged tiger removed from the wild is nothing more than a display of fur and some fangs, so too is a man untested by the world just a collection of muscles and some brains.

Listening to and accepting your animalistic urge is not an act worthy of shame, isolation, or embarrassment. It is not an emotion or sensation to ignore or be afraid of. It isn't an impulse you need to rein in and submerge. This urge is an essence you can harness, cultivate, and direct. It is an energy and life force that enhances and defines you. Embrace it.

This book has been written for Amazon distribution only. If you have enjoyed the text and wish to help others find it and benefit from it, the best thing you can do is to give this book a review on the site. The review helps with search results and guides people to make a more correct decision with their time. If you are interested in more of my writing, you can search for some of my other titles like Elite Tennis: A Guide, and Clash of Tennis Personalities. Thank you!

Made in the USA
San Bernardino, CA
15 January 2020